How to Draw Wolves (This Book Shows You How to Draw 32 Different Wolves Step by Step and is a Suitable How to Draw Wolves Book for Beginners)

This book will show you how to draw a range of wolves in different positions

James Manning

How to Draw Wolves

Introduction for Parents

Drawing is an essential part of a child's development, stimulating parts of the brain that are responsible for creative thinking and imagination. From a young age, we are all creatively encouraged to draw, whether it be at home or pre-school. Drawing is often encouraged to improve our fine motor skills and hand-eye co-ordination; this co-ordination is vital for future academic success and for improving our penmanship/handwriting skills.

From toddler's 'scribbles' to more refined 'matchstick men' and recognisable shapes, you may find that as your child grows they will want to tackle a more complex way of drawing (perhaps it's an image they have seen in a book) but as they begin to put pencil to paper they may have no idea where to start, causing frustration and annoyance.

With the help of our 'How to Draw' book series, this frustration will disappear as we guide your child step by step, line by line, to create their very own masterpiece!

Each illustration is deconstructed and simplified into lines and shapes which will not overwhelm your child. As we guide them to form each simple line and shape together on the paper, the image gradually becomes more detailed, textured and visually appealing. Practice will always make perfect, so encouraging your child to repeat the initial steps will incite a sense of self assurance that they are able to improve their skill line by line.

If Your Child Struggles With This Book

The rate of cognitive development varies from child to child and, as such, where one child may be ready for this book another will not. If you feel that your child is not ready for this book at the moment, take it away and bring it back to them in six to twelve months.

If your child is not ready to draw step-by-step, he or she may prefer to work using grids. Grid drawing involves copying information from one grid to another using coordinates. The type of copying required in grid drawing is very useful for the brain as, in particular, it exercises working memory. Working memory involves holding onto information temporarily and then using that temporarily held information at the same time. Working memory is an important process required in maintaining attention and exercising it will be beneficial for a range of activities, including in class at school.

Dr James Manning
Consultant Clinical Psychologist

For the webpage and password for your bonus books please see bottom of page 40.

HOW TO DRAW WOLVES

Here are all of the drawings in this book. I guess it must seem like there is a lot of them when they are looked at all at once!

Luckily, I am not going to ask you to draw them all straight away. The best way to learn to draw is one step at a time. Each drawing in this book may require between 50 and 200 strokes of your pencil, but all you will need to think about is drawing one stroke at a time.

As you use your pencil, stroke by stroke, working your way through this book, you will eventually be able to create all of the drawings!

Drawing Step-by-Step

In this book I will show you how to create 32 different drawings step by step. Each step will build on the previous one until eventually you have 32 complete drawings.

To make things easier for you, please download the outline grids for the drawings. You can download this additional book with all of them inside for free by visiting the web address below:

https://www.lipdf.com/product/wolves/

At first, you find my step-by-step approach too complicated or difficult please leave it to one side and come back to it later. Instead, you may want to use an alternative grid with numbers and letters on it first. By following the coordinates and matching them up with the coordinates on a blank grid you can redraw the pictures this way instead.

I have put details below about where you can download these basic grids for free on the internet.

https://www.lipdf.com/product/grids/

You can of course ask an adult to help you draw the grids instead, or you may even feel able to draw them yourself.

Please see page 40 for the webpage address for your bonus books and the password.

1.Although this is the first character in the book, you don't have to start drawing here! Flick through the book and find your favourite drawing to start with.

Suggested outline sketch

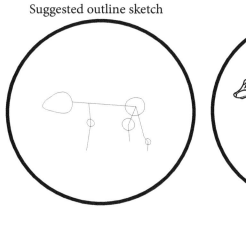

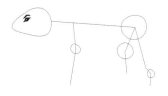

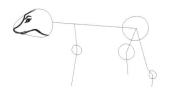

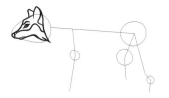

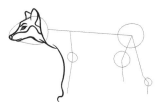

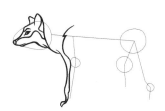

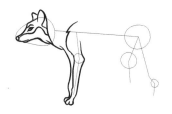

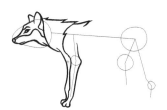

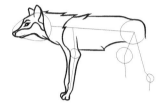
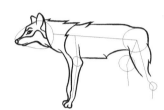

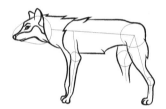
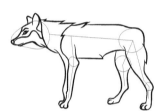
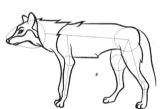

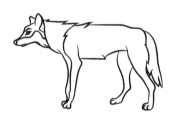

	A	B	C	D	E	F	G	H
1								
2								
3								
4								
5								
6								
7								
8								
9								
10								
11								
12								

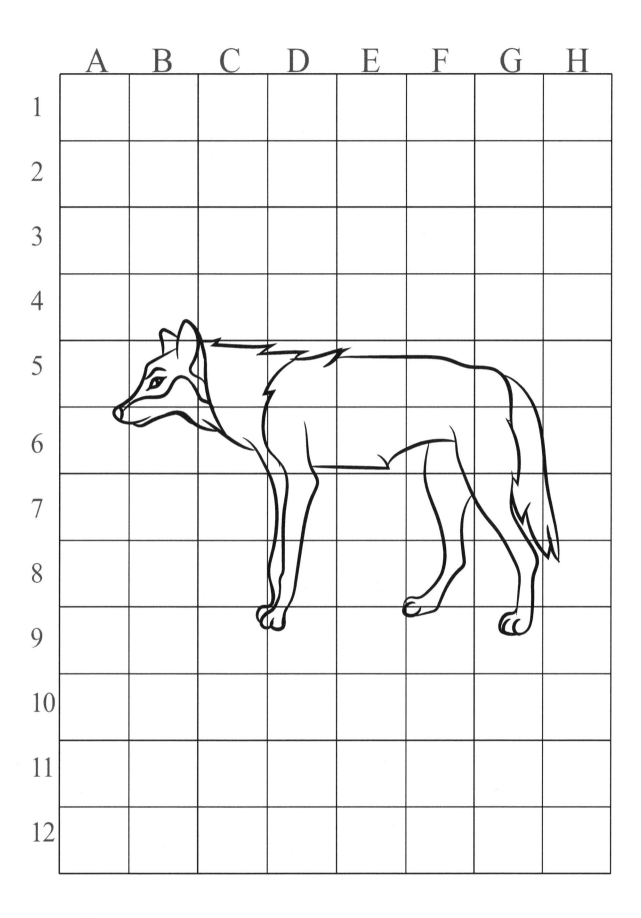

2. Keep practicing. It's often helpful if you use a pencil so you can erase anything you think is a mistake.

Suggested outline sketch

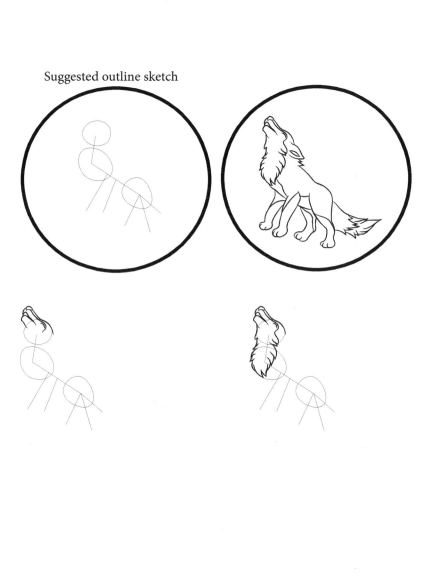

	A	B	C	D	E	F	G	H
1								
2								
3								
4								
5								
6								
7								
8								
9								
10								
11								
12								

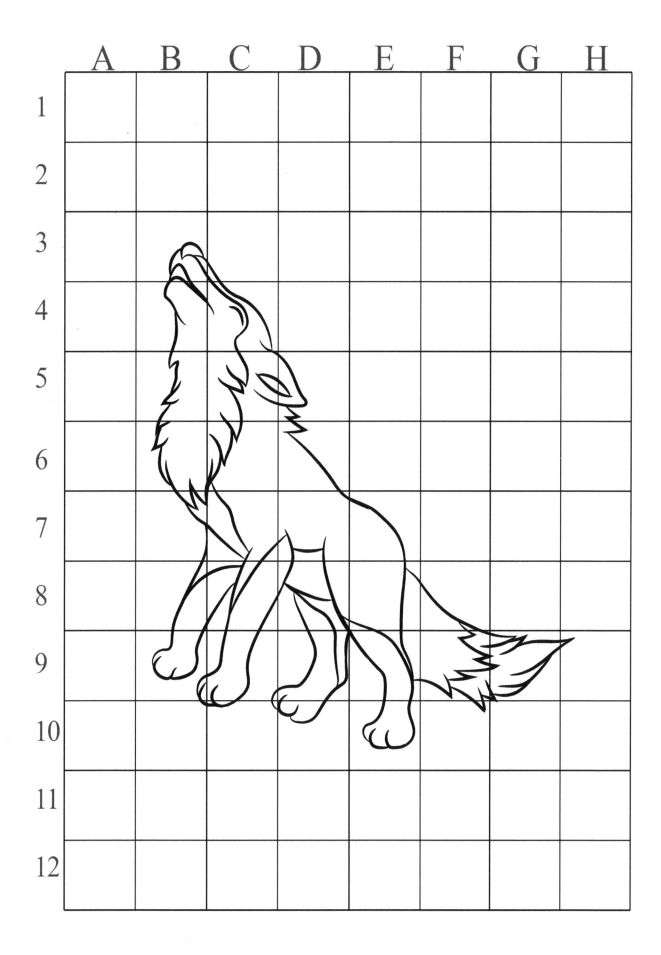

3. The first stroke of your pencil can often be the most daunting but give it a go and see where the drawing takes you!

Suggested outline sketch

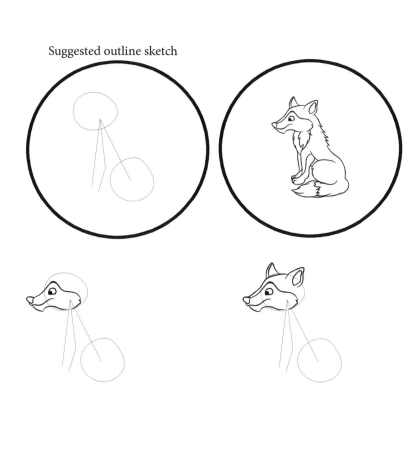

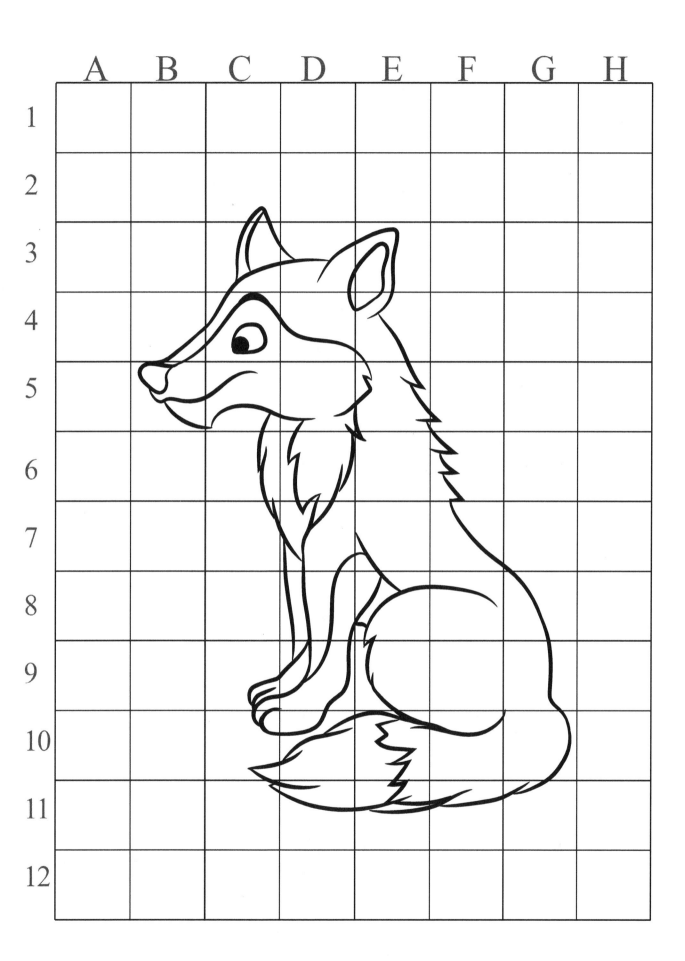

	A	B	C	D	E	F	G	H
1								
2								
3								
4								
5								
6								
7								
8								
9								
10								
11								
12								

4. Copying the lines exactly as they are shown in the book isn't a necessity, use the grids as a guide and source of inspiration for your own drawing.

Suggested outline sketch

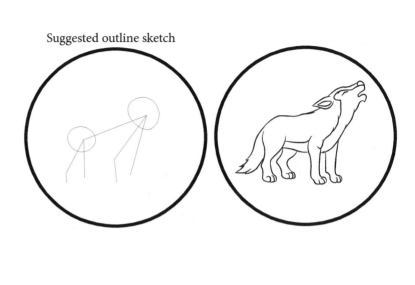

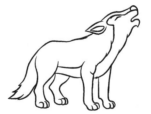

	A	B	C	D	E	F	G	H

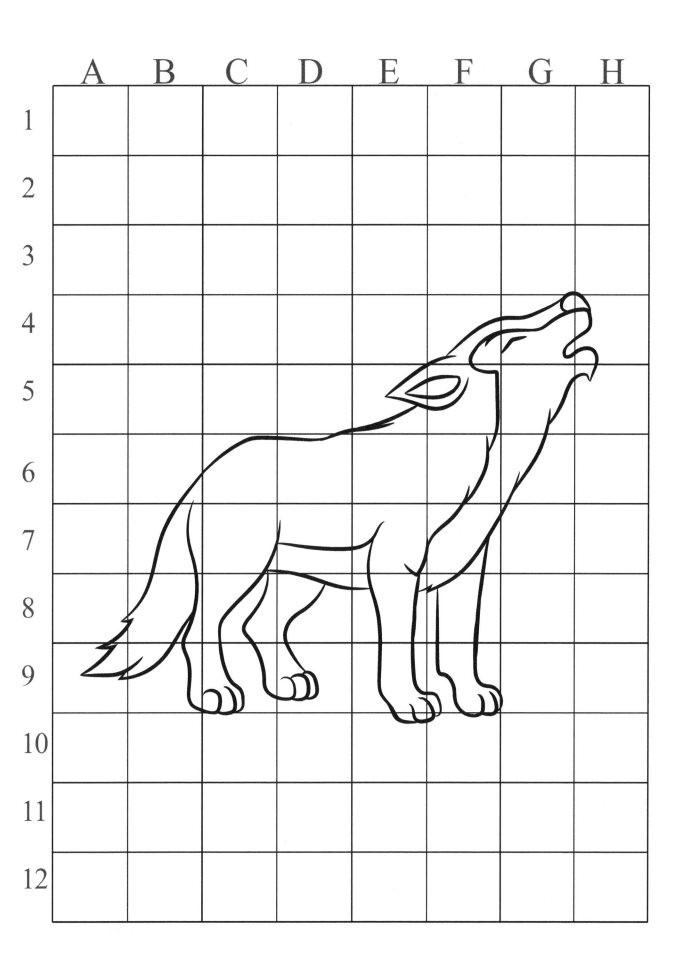

5. Don't get frustrated if you can't copy the lines exactly, just use them to point you in the right direction.

Suggested outline sketch

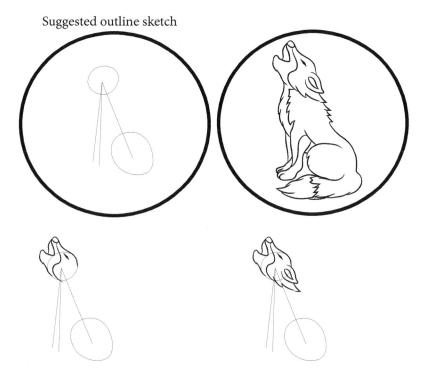

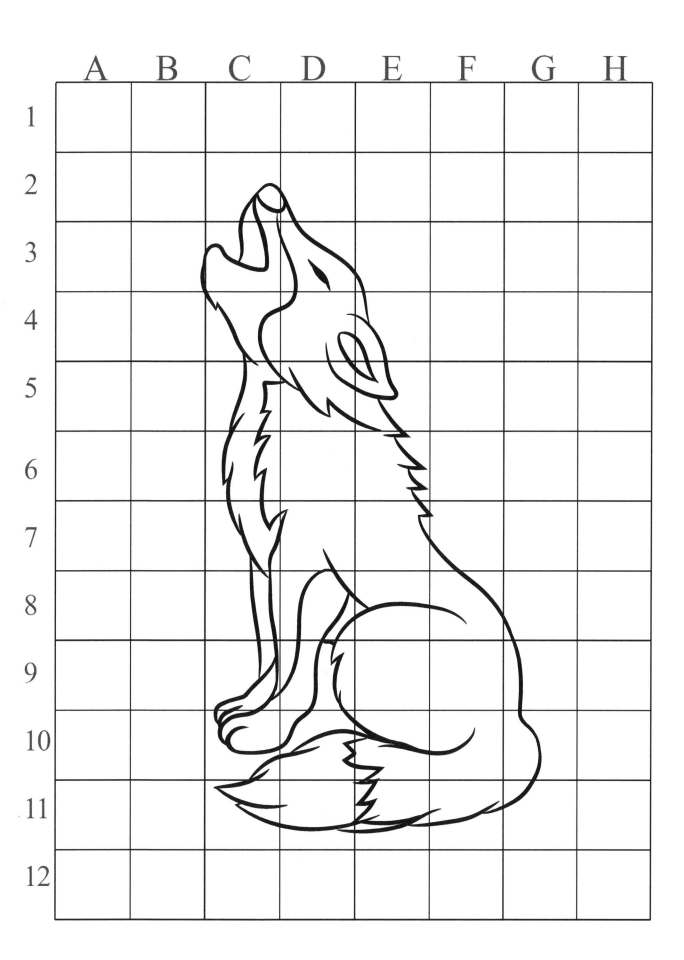

6. If you find you are getting frustrated with your drawing, take a break and come back to it later.

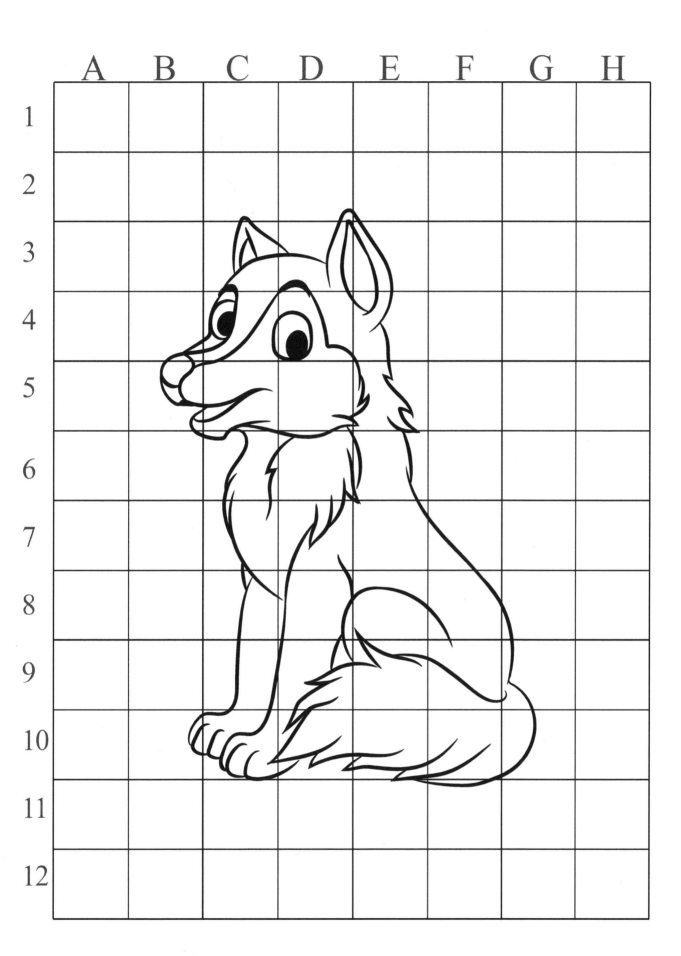

7. Don't worry if you are spending more time drawing a picture, it's more important to take your time when producing high quality work.

Suggested outline sketch

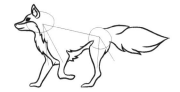  

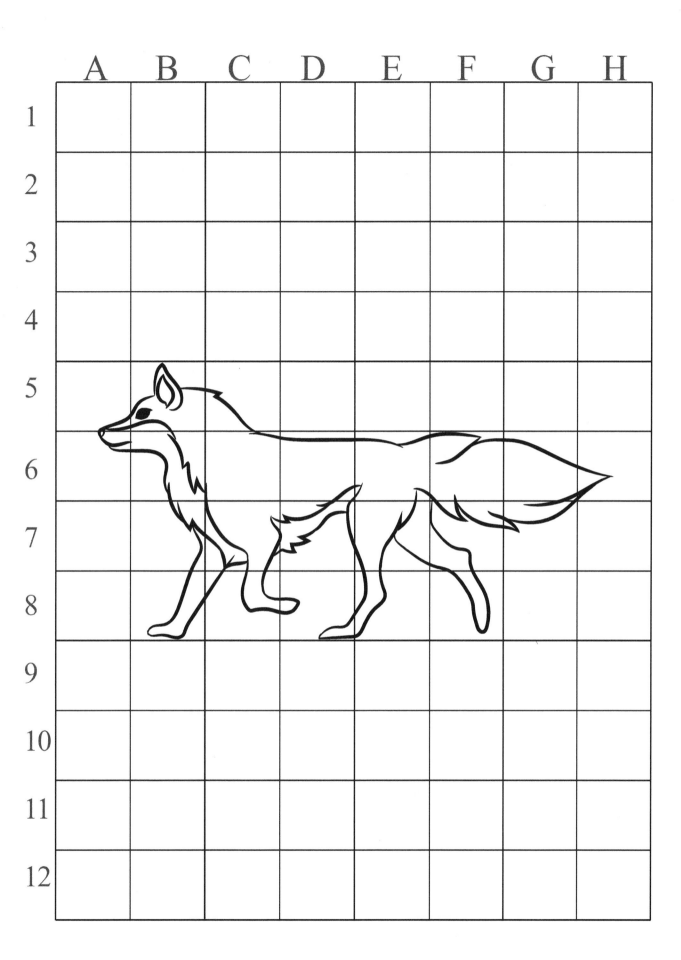

8. Try not to worry about how your character looks at this stage, once you have drawn in the other parts it will bring them to life!

Suggested outline sketch

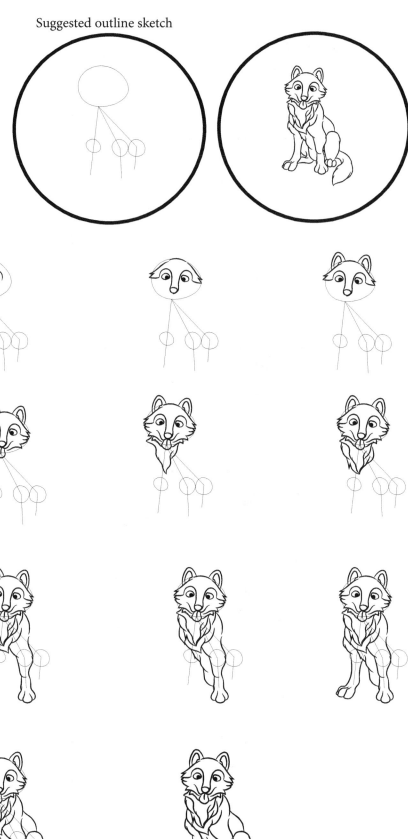

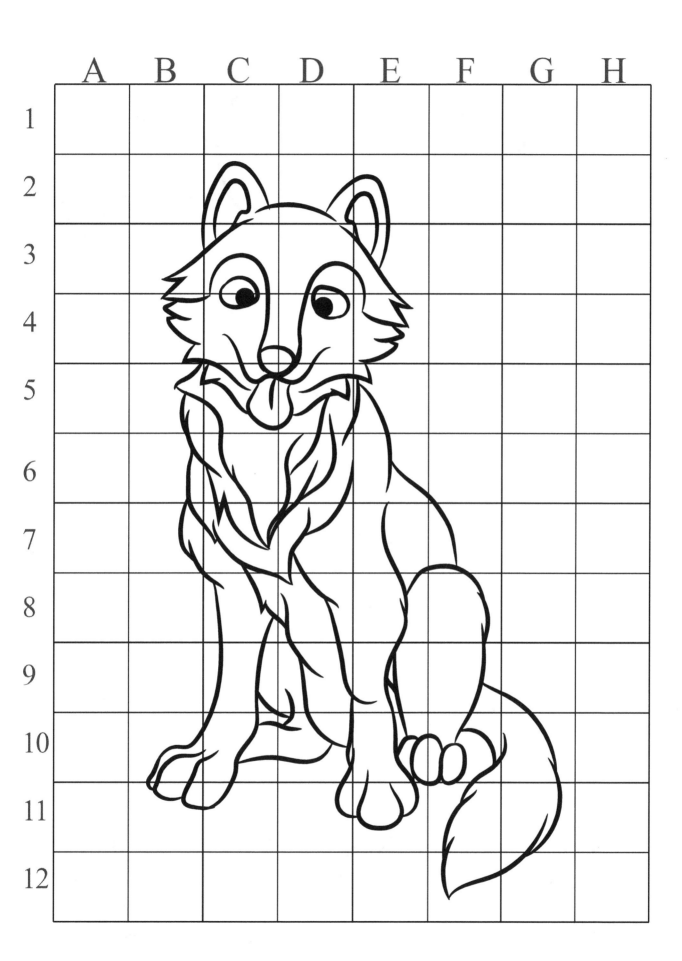

	A	B	C	D	E	F	G	H
1								
2								
3								
4								
5								
6								
7								
8								
9								
10								
11								
12								

9. Don't rush through the pages of this book, take your time to ensure high quality drawing.

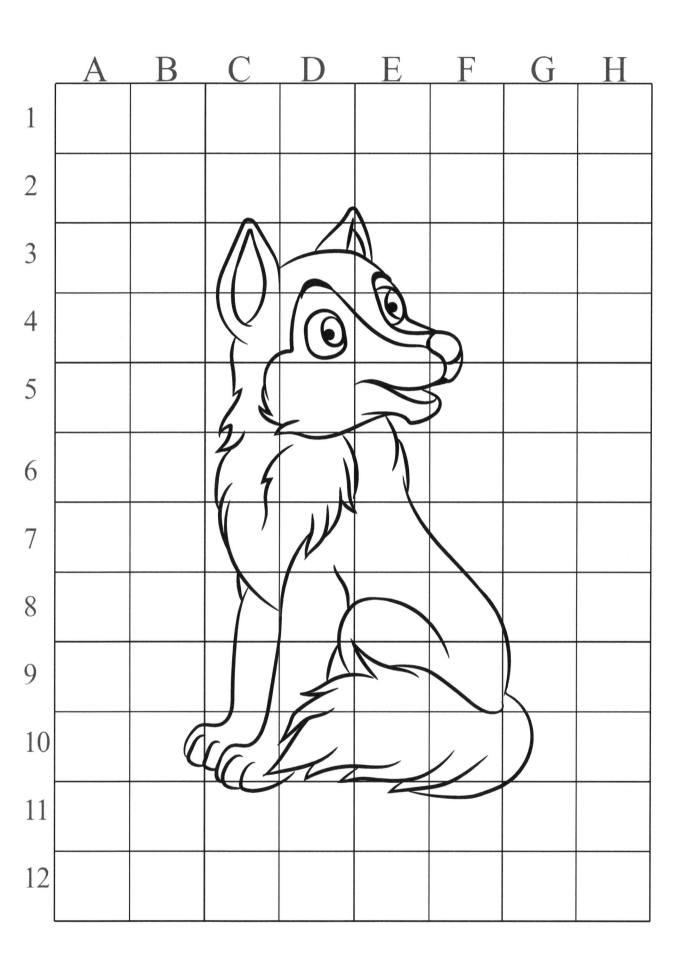

	A	B	C	D	E	F	G	H
1								
2								
3								
4								
5								
6								
7								
8								
9								
10								
11								
12								

10. A simple change such as moving the characters pupils in their eyes can make them seem like they are looking at something.

Suggested outline sketch

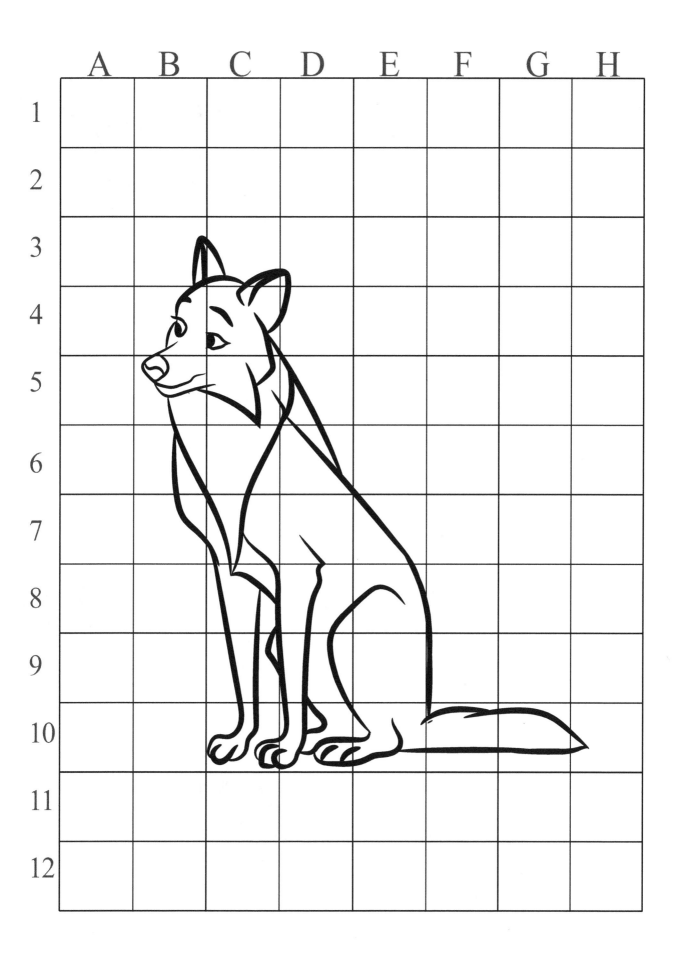

11. Start with a simple outline and build your character from there.

Suggested outline sketch

	A	B	C	D	E	F	G	H
1								
2								
3								
4								
5								
6								
7								
8								
9								
10								
11								
12								

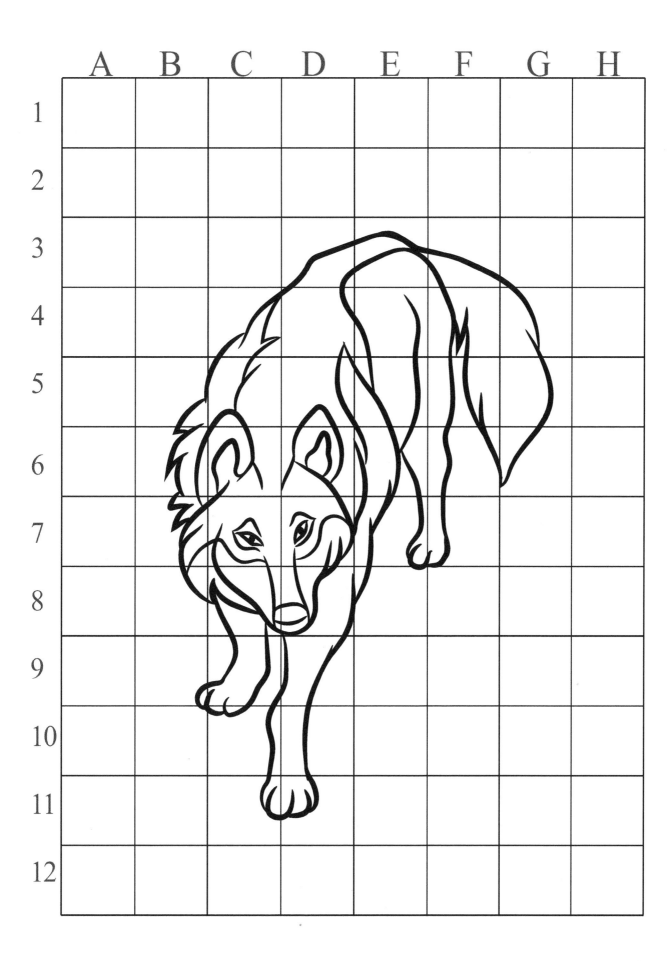

12. Have a go at colouring in your drawing once it's finished!

Suggested outline sketch

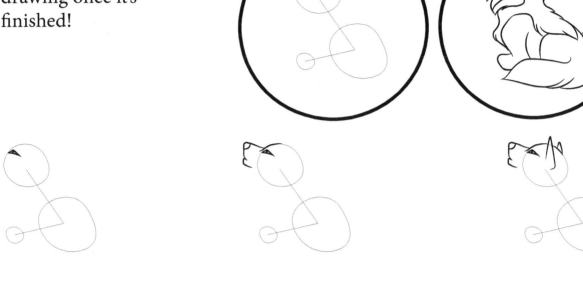

	A	B	C	D	E	F	G	H
1								
2								
3								
4								
5								
6								
7								
8								
9								
10								
11								
12								

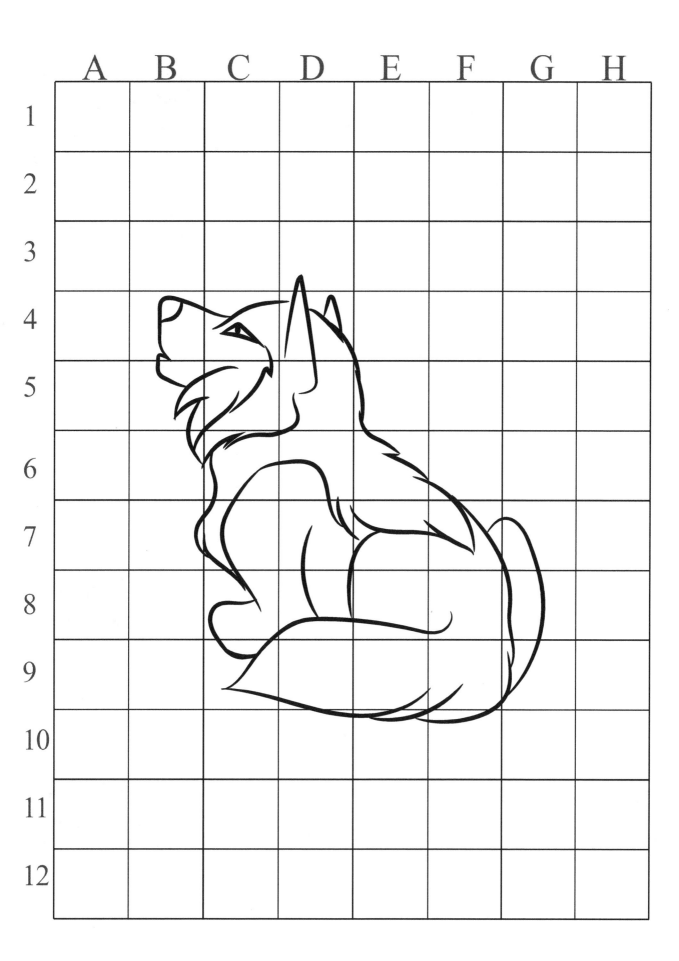

13. If you find you are drawing the head too small and are struggling to draw in all the features, try starting your drawing with the eyes and mouth, then draw in the shape of the head afterwards.

Suggested outline sketch

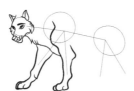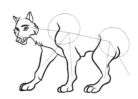

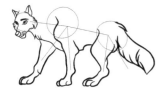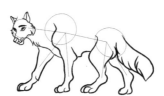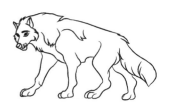

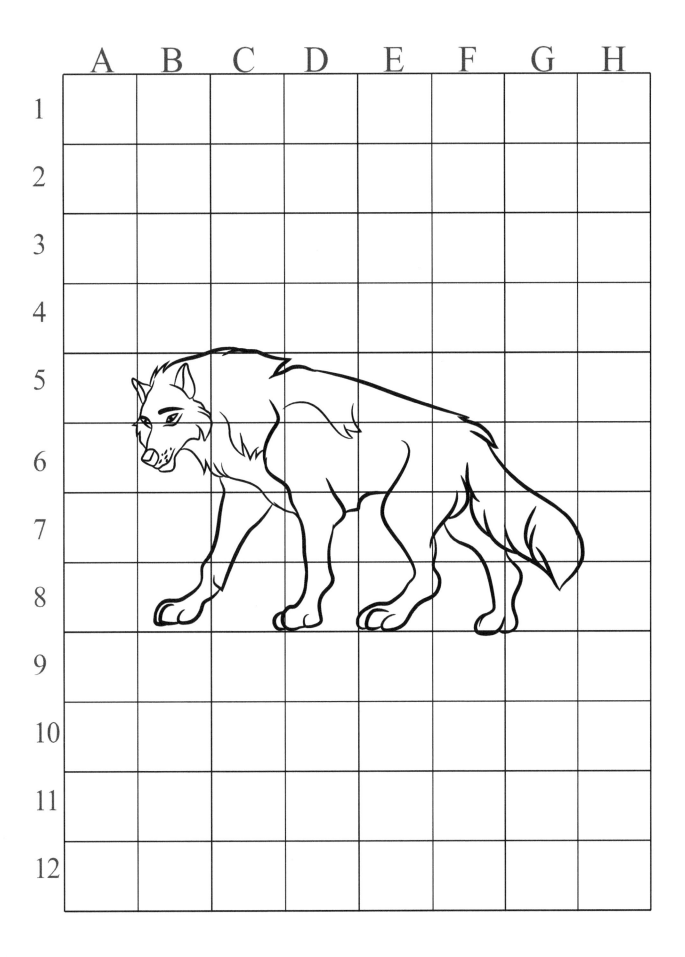

14. Add in extra features to make you drawing unique and personal to you.

Suggested outline sketch

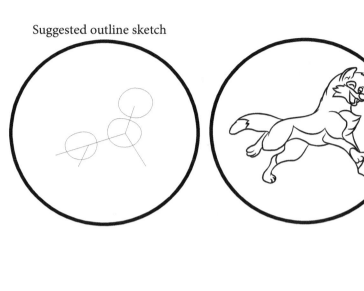

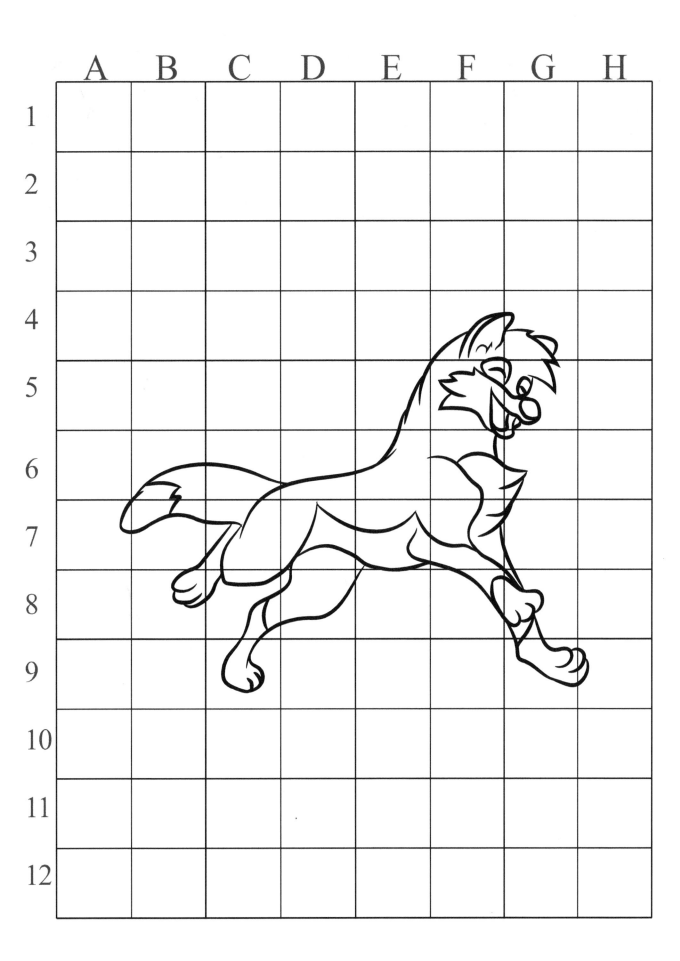

	A	B	C	D	E	F	G	H
1								
2								
3								
4								
5								
6								
7								
8								
9								
10								
11								
12								

15. Once you have practiced using grids, in the future you may be able to create your drawing from memory alone.

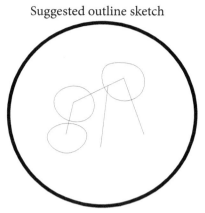

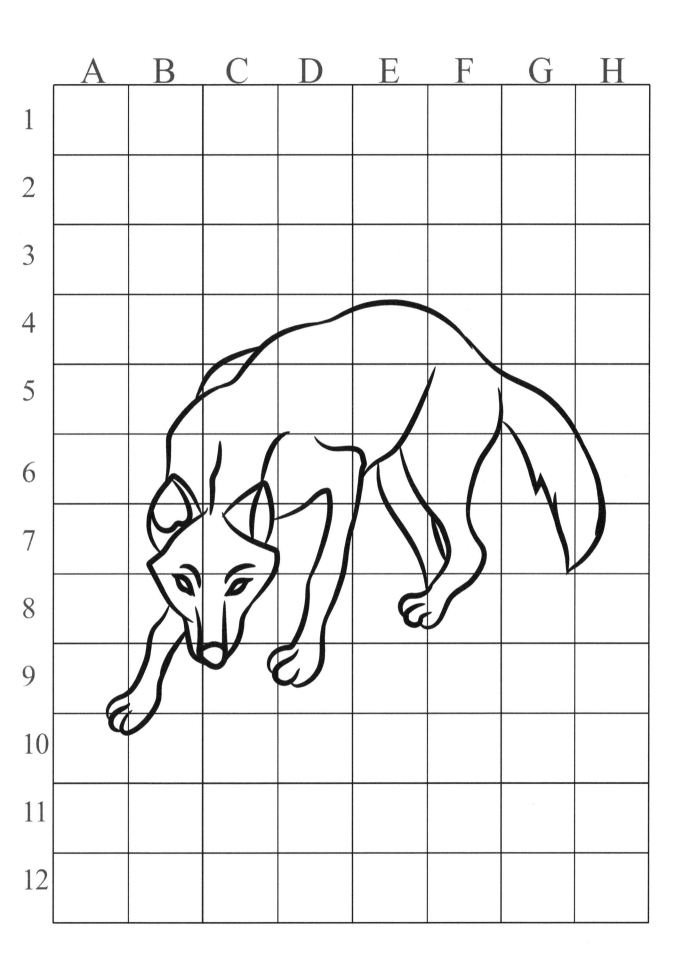

	A	B	C	D	E	F	G	H
1								
2								
3								
4								
5								
6								
7								
8								
9								
10								
11								
12								

16. It's unlikely you will get everything right the first time. Draw in pencil so you can erase any mistakes.

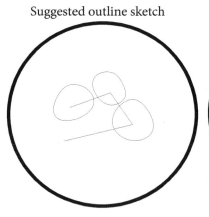

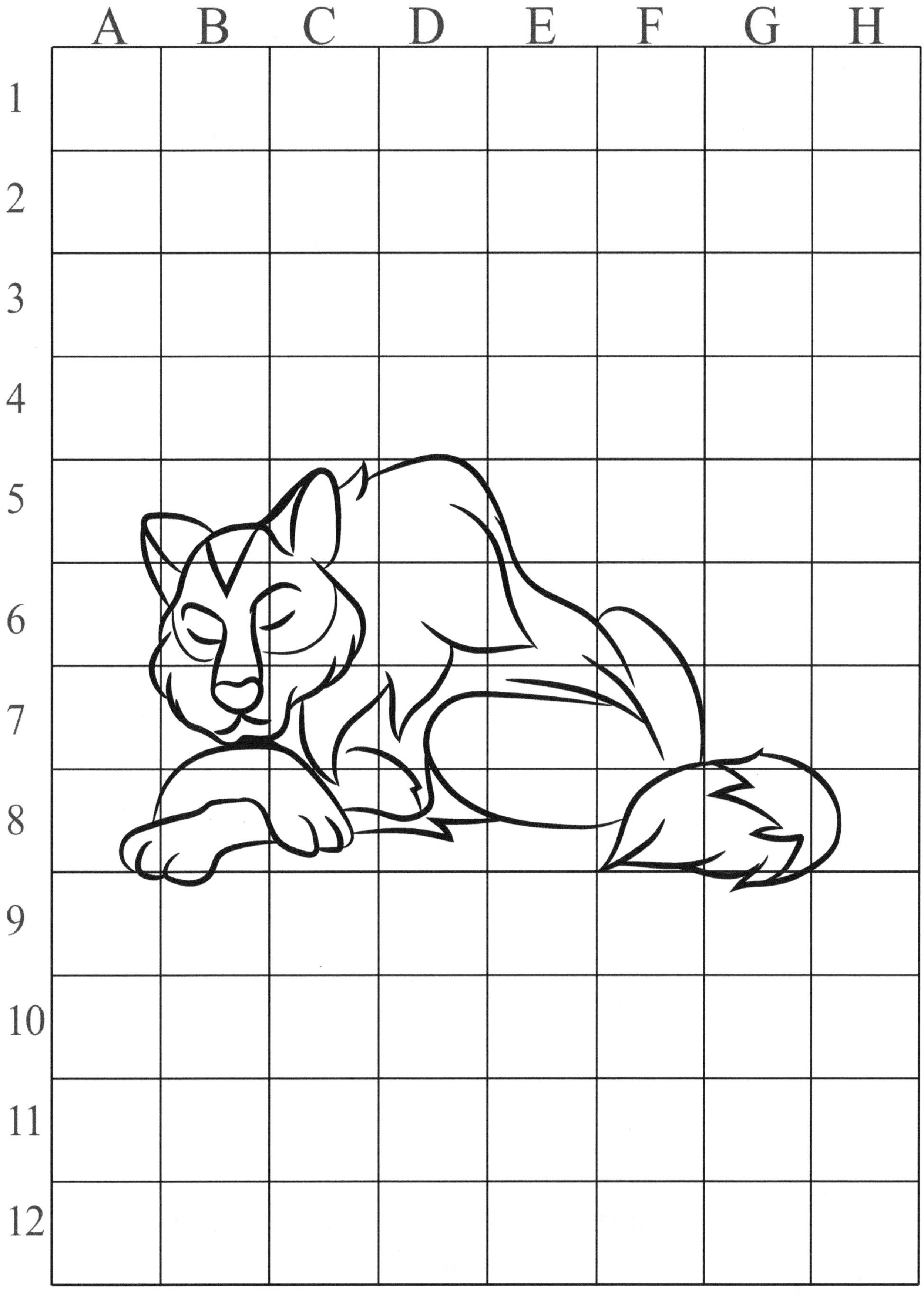
A B C D E F G H
1
2
3
4
5
6
7
8
9
10
11
12

17. Why not experiment with how you hold your pencil? How you hold a pen for handwriting may not be comfortable for drawing.

Suggested outline sketch

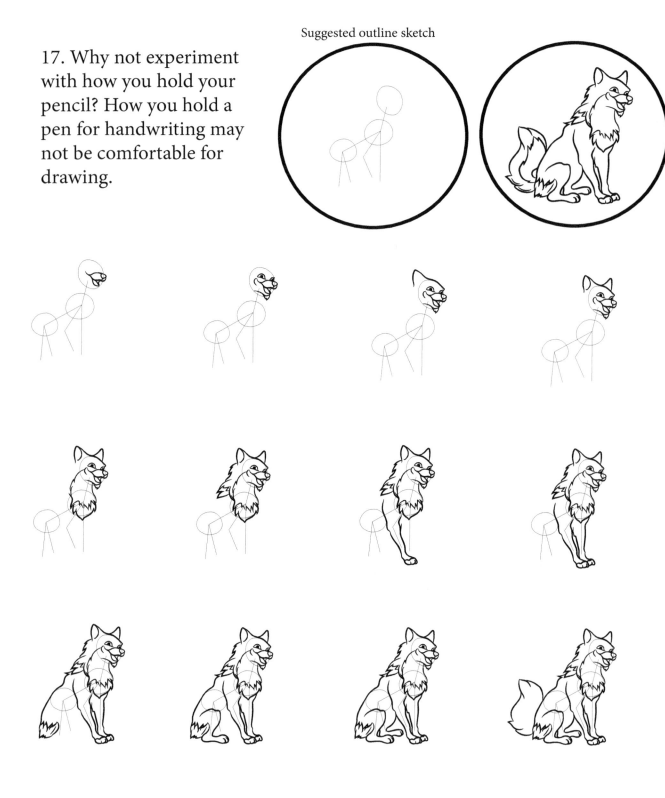

	A	B	C	D	E	F	G	H
1								
2								
3								
4								
5								
6								
7								
8								
9								
10								
11								
12								

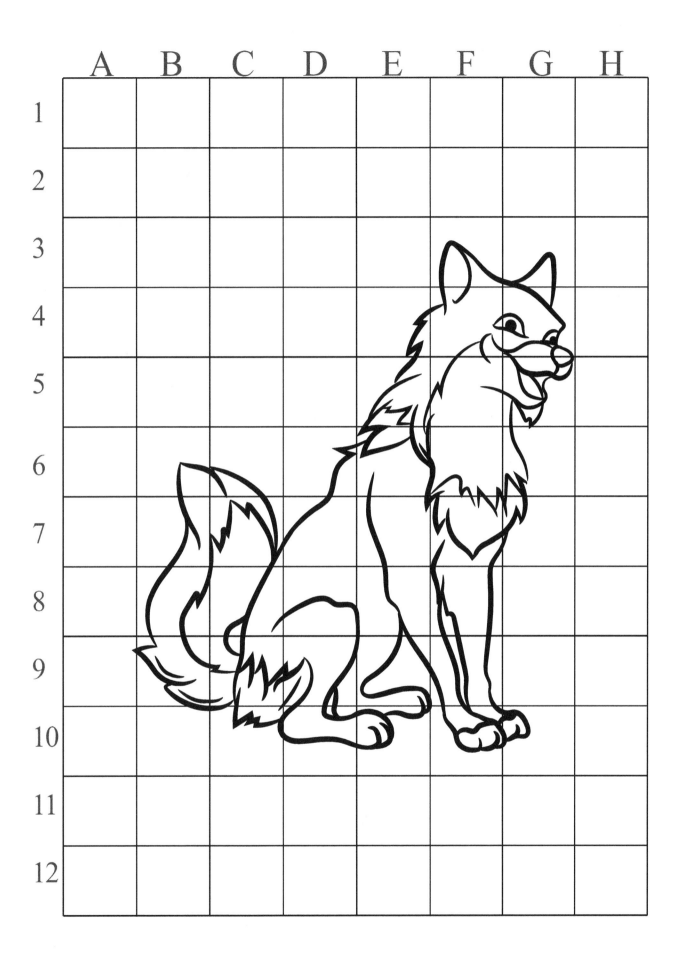

18. There are no rules with art. Feel free to interpret the drawing in your own style.

Suggested outline sketch

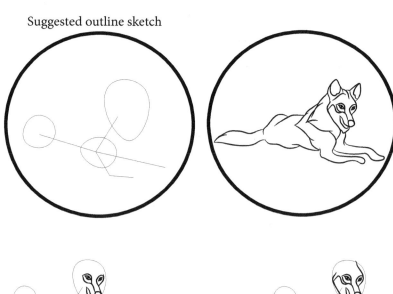

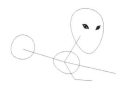

	A	B	C	D	E	F	G	H
1								
2								
3								
4								
5								
6								
7								
8								
9								
10								
11								
12								

19. Patience is key. If you are getting irritated with your work, leave it for now and come back to it later.

Suggested outline sketch

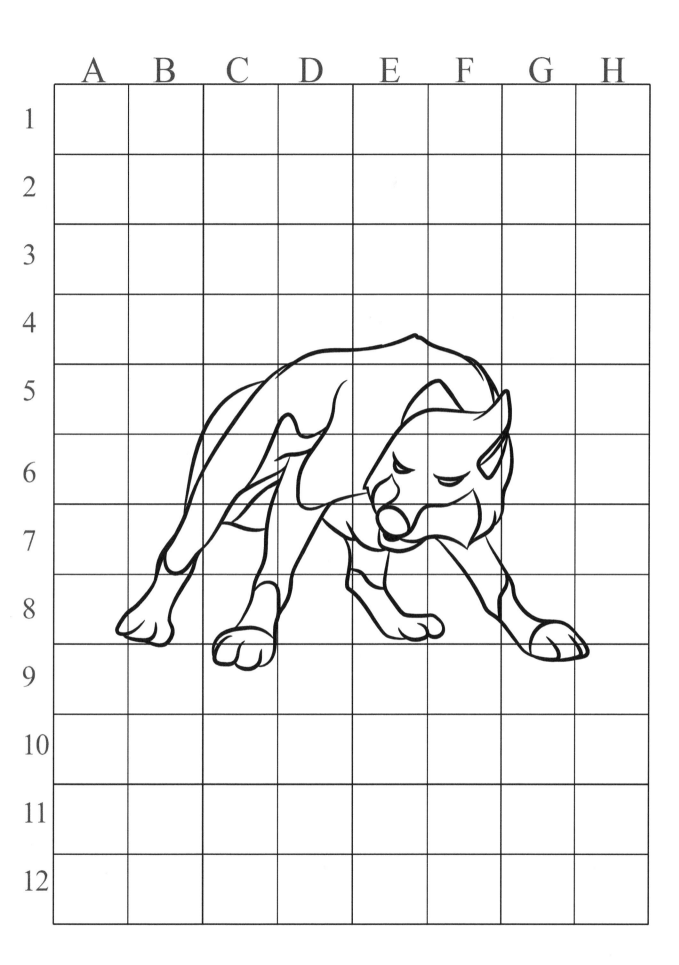

20. You could have a go at very roughly sketching out the shapes, then going over the lines in pen. Once finished, erase out the rough lines.

Suggested outline sketch

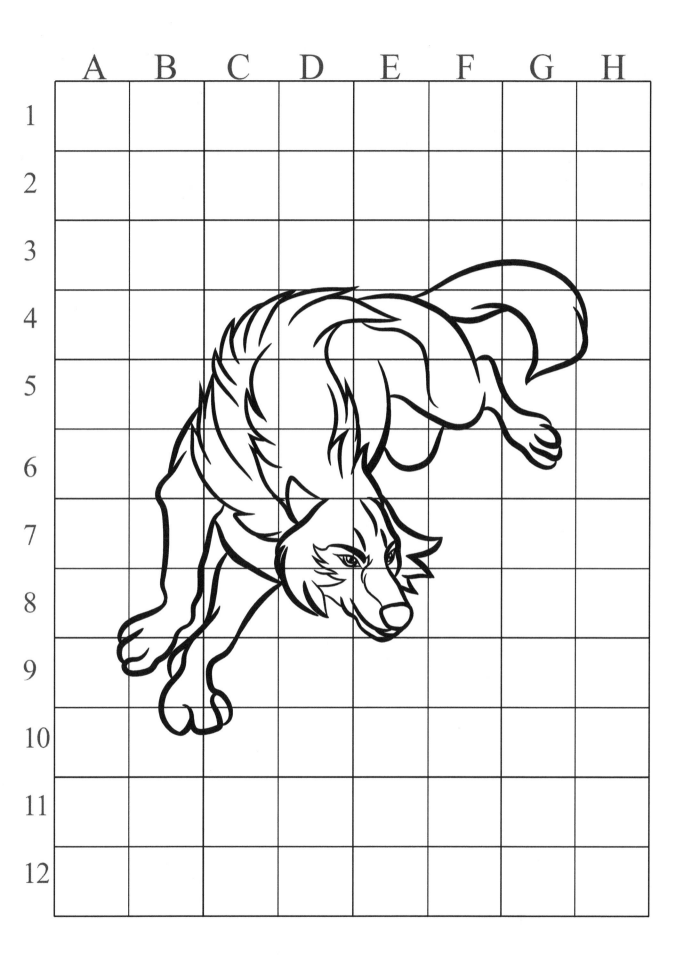

21. If you struggle with this particular drawing, stop where you are and try another page in this book. You can always come back to this page later.

Suggested outline sketch

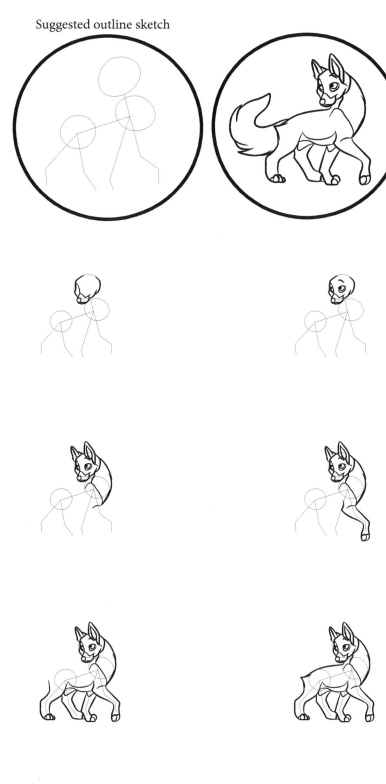

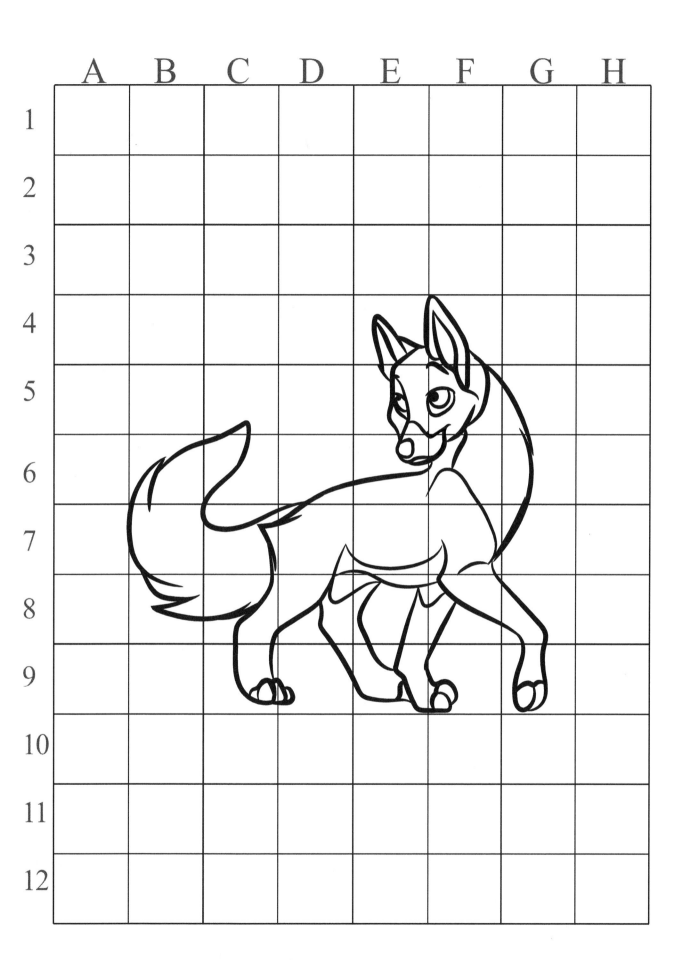

22. To give your brain a workout, complete a drawing in an opposite way to way you would normally approach it. Sometimes this can help us see things that we did not notice before.

Suggested outline sketch

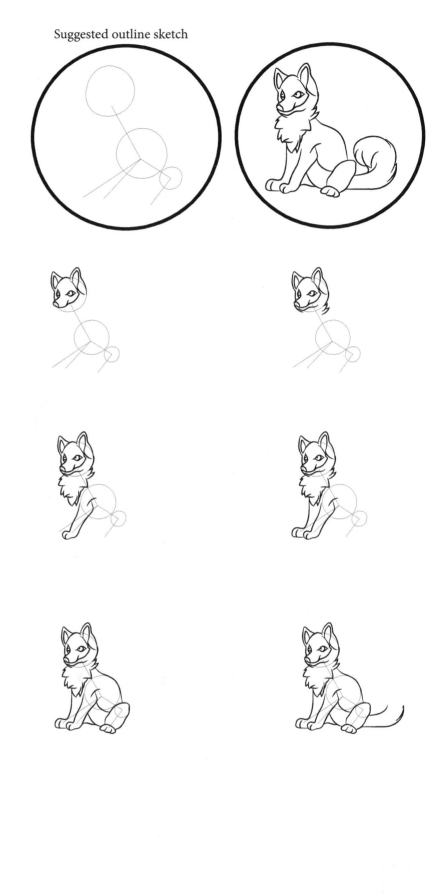

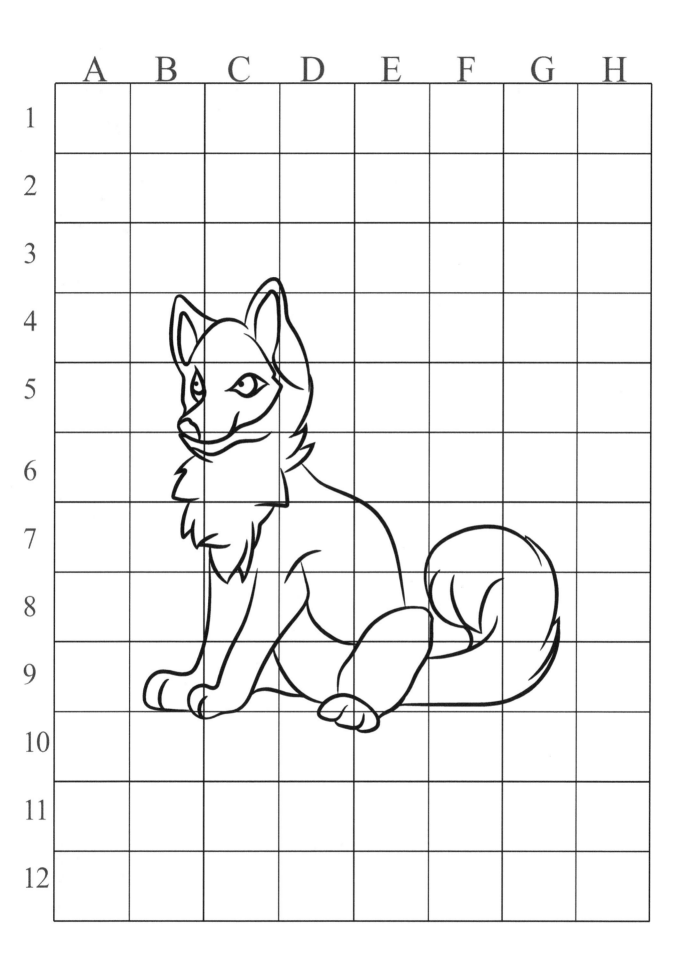

	A	B	C	D	E	F	G	H
1								
2								
3								
4								
5								
6								
7								
8								
9								
10								
11								
12								

23. Draw the head first and then build the rest of the body around it.

Suggested outline sketch

52

	A	B	C	D	E	F	G	H
1								
2								
3								
4								
5								
6								
7								
8								
9								
10								
11								
12								

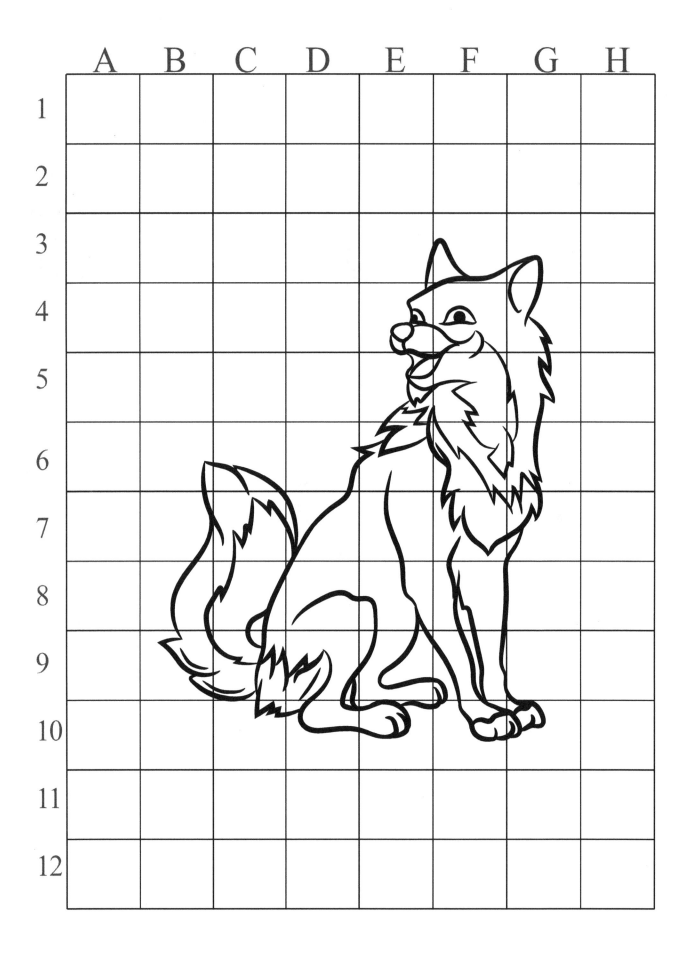

24. Starting your drawing with the eyes will help your initial sketch to take shape. Follow that by constructing the head.

Suggested outline sketch

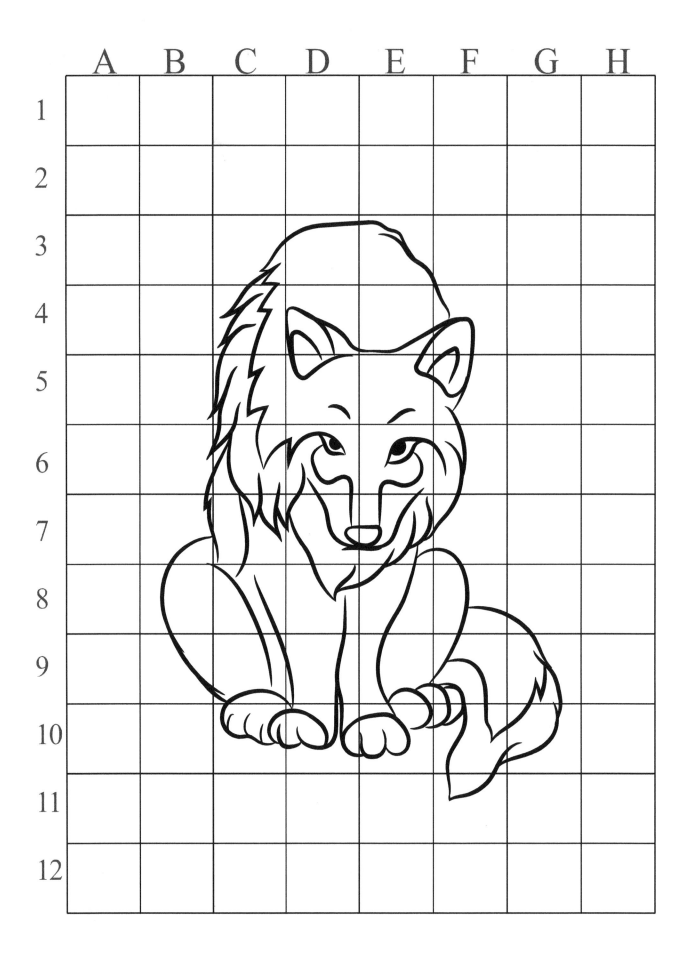

25. Separate your initial sketch into sections to help you decide how you want to proportion your drawing. This can help you to alter the height of your character.

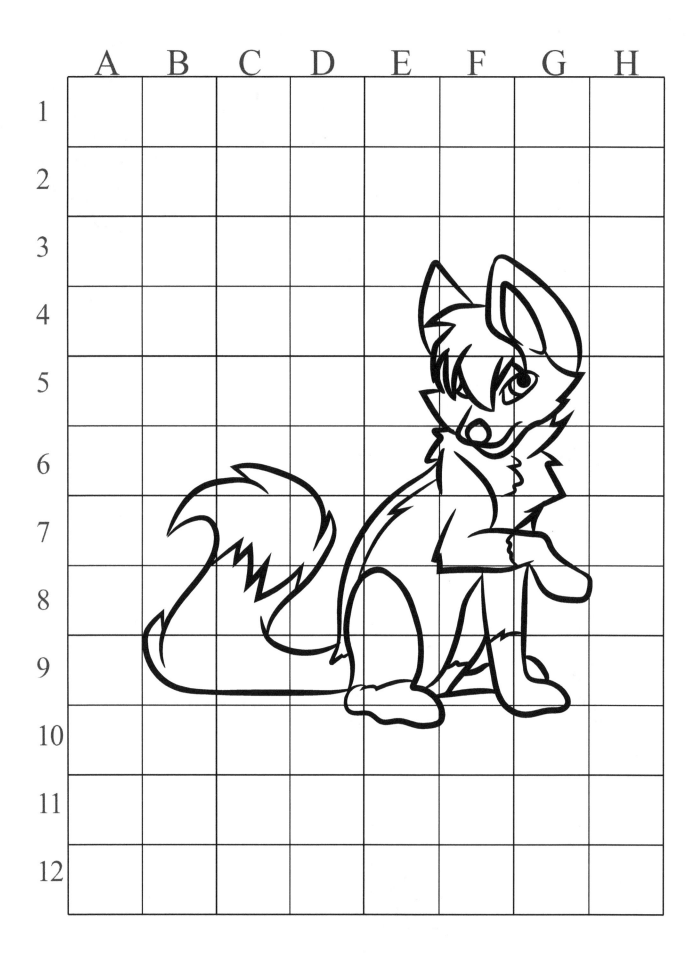

26. The use of ellipses in grids can be very helpful when you want to create round shapes. You can change the features of your character by lengthening some parts and shortening others.

Suggested outline sketch

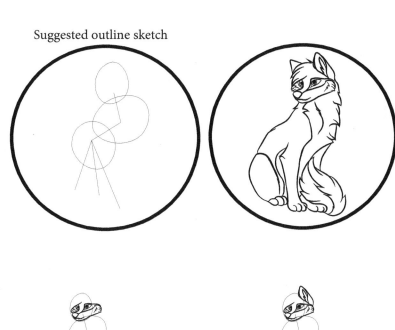

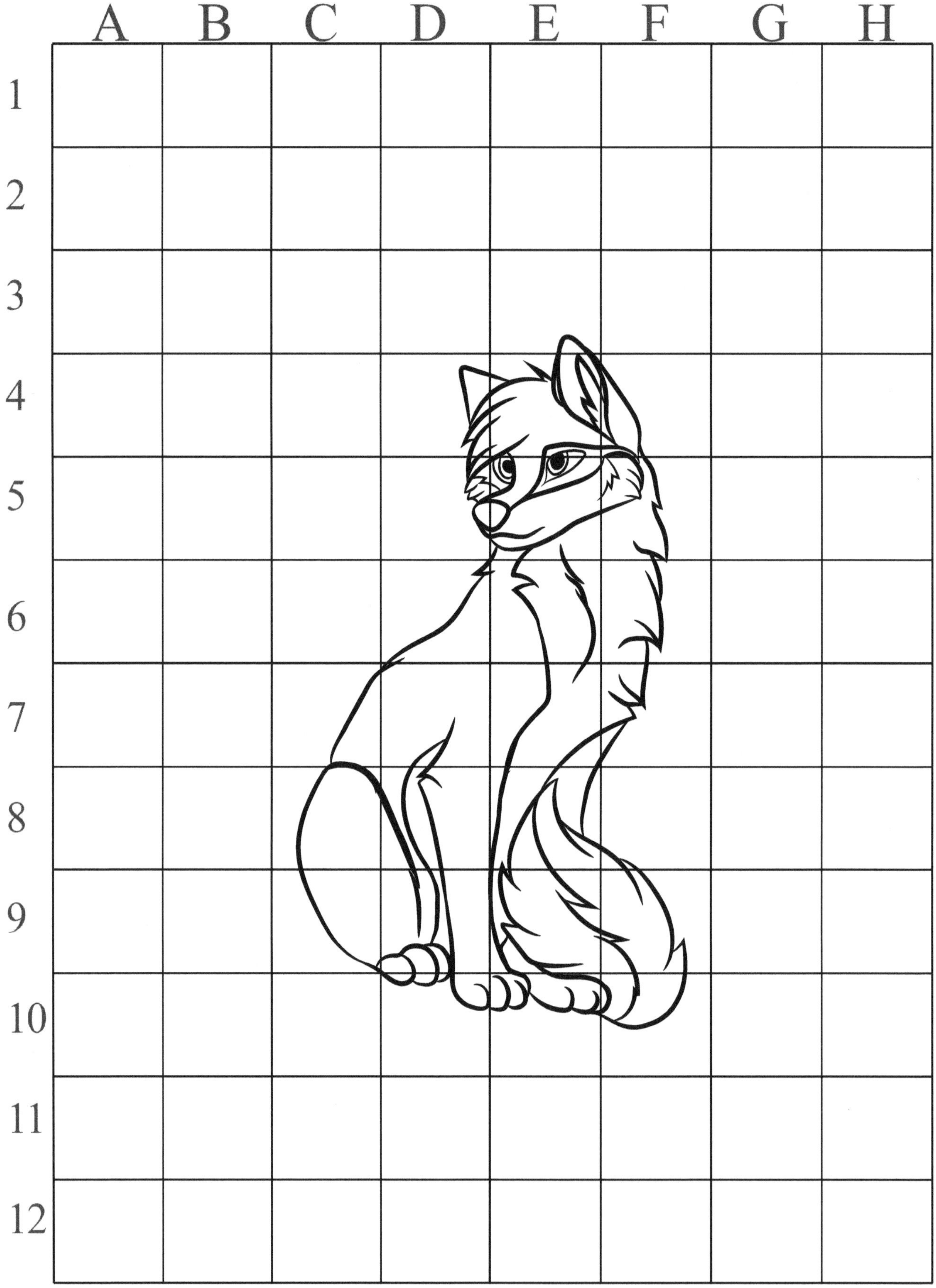
A B C D E F G H
1
2
3
4
5
6
7
8
9
10
11
12

27. A simple outline sketch can often help to guide you when drawing. After you have drawn your grid, begin with the eyes. Try changing your character's features to create alternative versions.

Suggested outline sketch

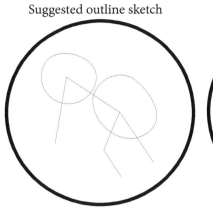

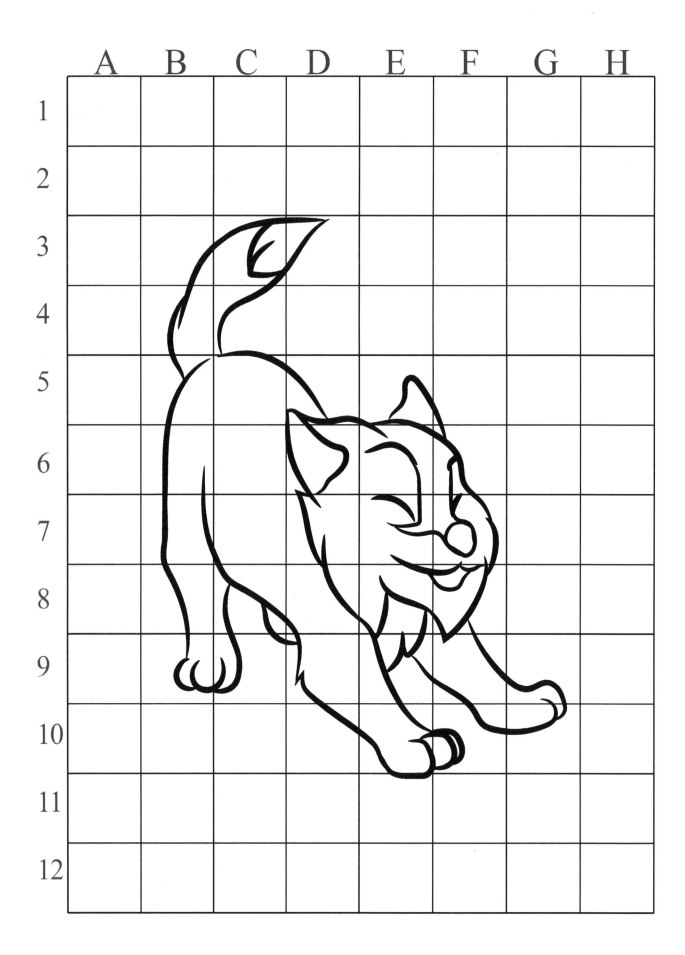

27. A simple outline sketch can often help to guide you when drawing. After you have drawn your grid, begin with the eyes. Try changing your character's features to create alternative versions.

Suggested outline sketch

	A	B	C	D	E	F	G	H
1								
2								
3								
4								
5								
6								
7								
8								
9								
10								
11								
12								

29. You can make your character's head stand out more by creating a larger area of overlap on your ellipses.

Suggested outline sketch

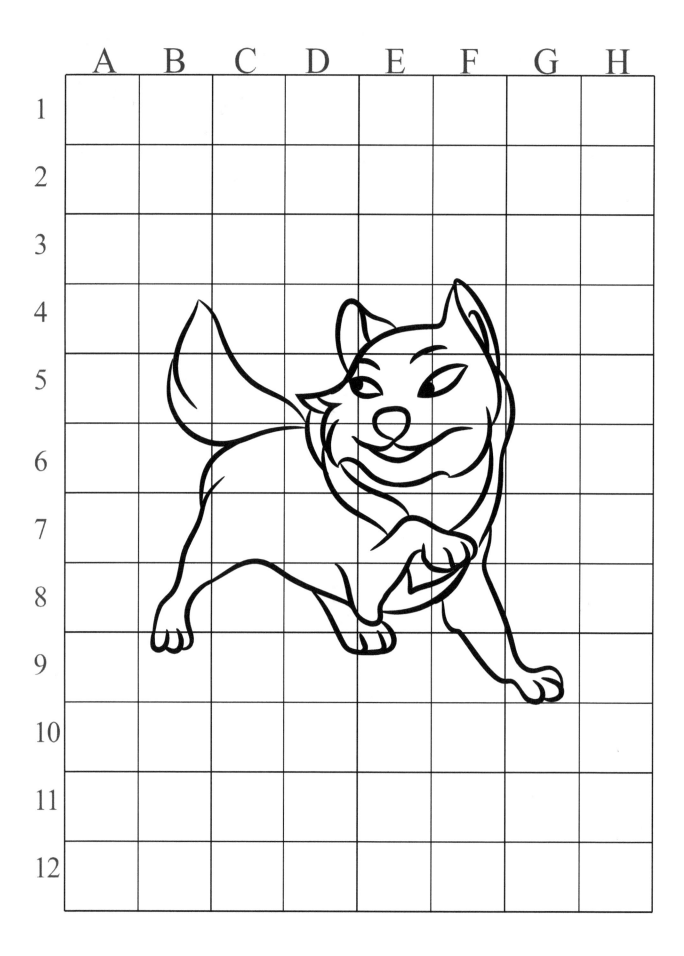

30. After you have sketched out this drawing step by step, add extra features to make it look more original or personal to you.

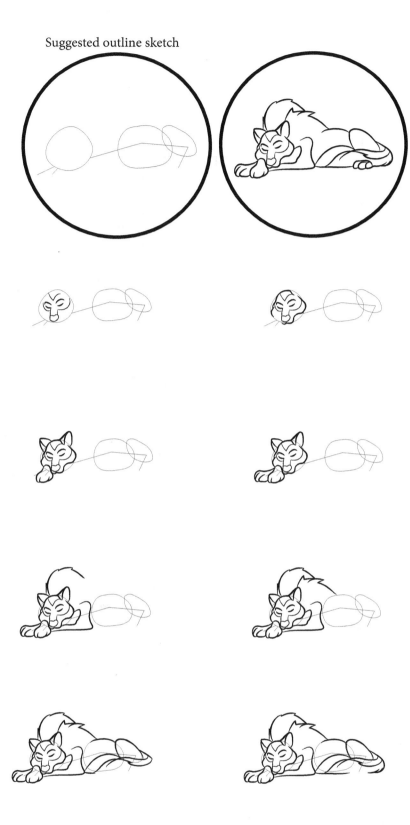

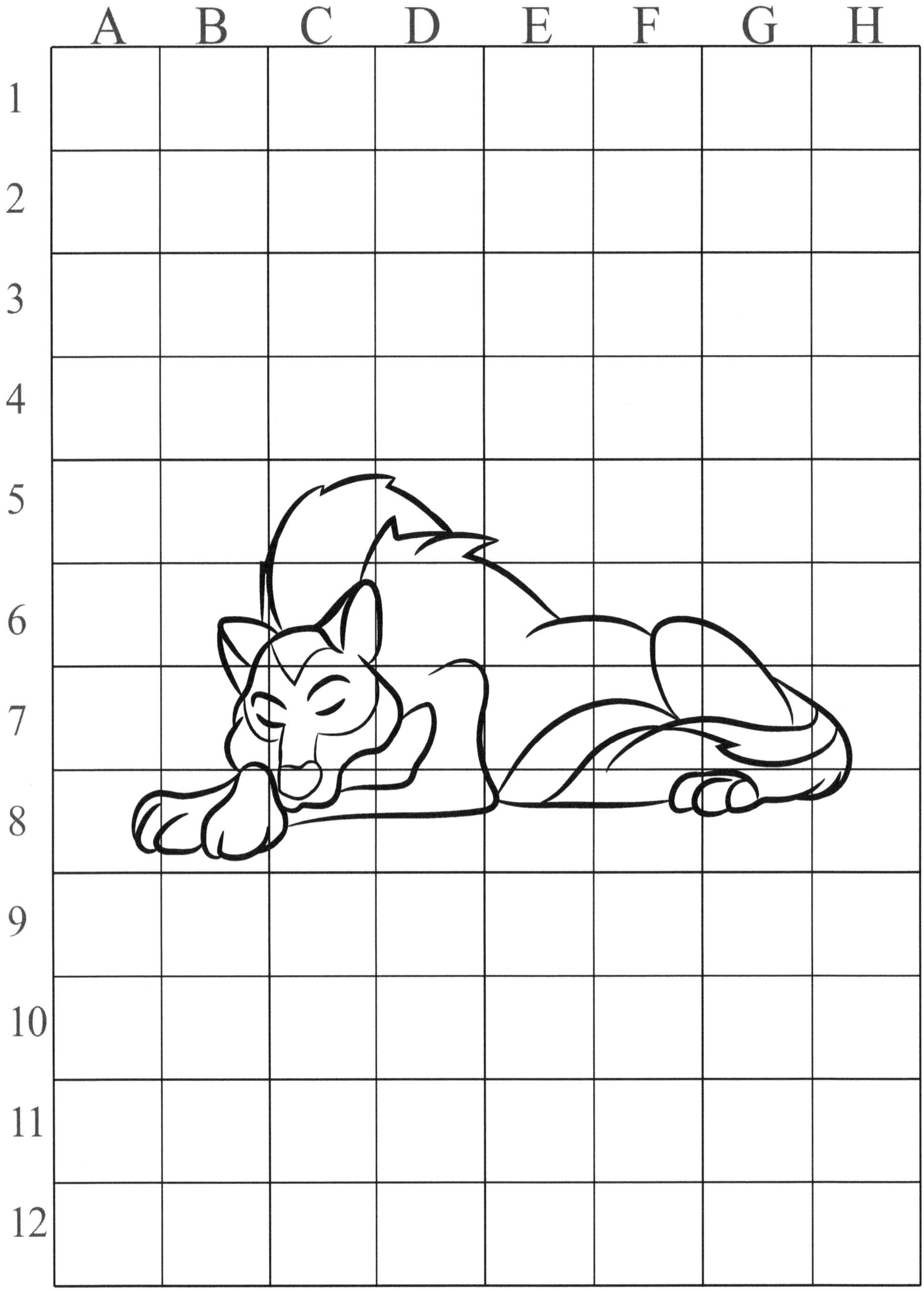
A B C D E F G H
1
2
3
4
5
6
7
8
9
10
11
12

31. Ask questions to stimulate your creativity. Following this, listen to the suggestions your mind comes up with.

Suggested outline sketch

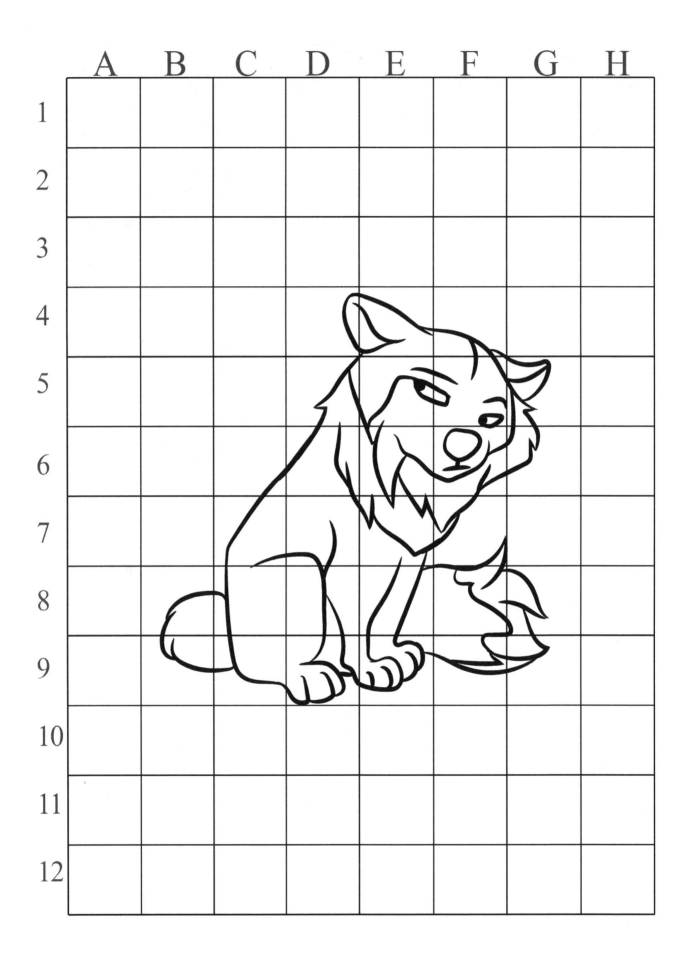

32. Anthropomorphism occurs when you give your non-human character human-like characteristics.

Suggested outline sketch

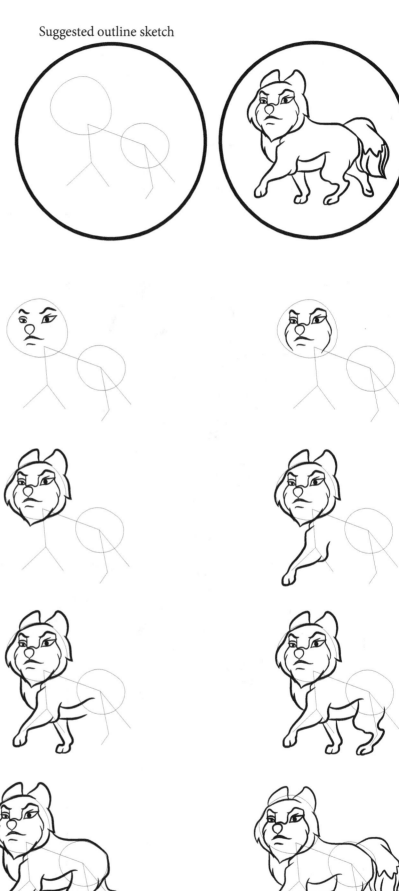

	A	B	C	D	E	F	G	H
1								
2								
3								
4								
5								
6								
7								
8								
9								
10								
11								
12								

CPSIA information can be obtained
at www.ICGtesting.com
Printed in the USA
LVHW061916091121
702880LV00006B/69